Farm Animals

DK

Penguin Random House

Project editor **James Mitchem**
Editorial assistant **Sophia Danielsson-Waters**
Senior designer **Claire Patané**
Designer **Charlotte Bull**
Design assistants **Eleanor Bates, Rachael Hare**
Photographer **Ruth Jenkinson**
Producer **Leila Green**
Producer, Pre-Production **Andy Hilliard**
Jacket designer **Charlotte Bull**
Jacket coordinator **Francesca Young**
Creative technical support **Sonia Charbonnier**
Managing editor **Penny Smith**
Managing art editor **Gemma Glover**
Art director **Jane Bull**
Publisher **Mary Ling**

First published in Great Britain in 2016 by
Dorling Kindersley Limited
80 Strand, London WC2R 0RL

Copyright © 2016 Dorling Kindersley Limited
A Penguin Random House Company
10 9 8 7 6 5 4 3 2 1
001–288476–Mar/16

A CIP catalogue record for this book is available
from the British Library.
ISBN: 978–0–2412–3833–2
Printed in China.
All images © Dorling Kindersley Limited
For further information see: www.dkimages.com

A WORLD OF IDEAS
SEE ALL THERE IS TO KNOW

www.dk.com

Parents

This booked is packed with
activities for your little ones to
enjoy. We want you all to have
a great time, but please be
safe and sensible – especially
when you're doing anything
that might *be* dangerous
(or messy!) Have fun.

1

2

3

Contents

Who lives on the farm?

The farm is a place to find lots and lots of **friendly animals**. Do you have a favourite?

Chickens

Cluck cluck! Chicken lay lots of yummy eggs.

Ducks

Quack quack! Ducks can fly, swim, and dive underwater.

Cows

Moooo! Cows spend almost all day chewing on grass!

It's fun to live on the farm

Can you spot the mouse?

Pigs

Oink oink! Playful pigs roll in the mud to keep cool in the hot sun.

Sheep

Baaaaa! Sheep have thick woolly coats.

Horses

Neigh! Horses can pull carts and do other jobs on a farm.

Goats

Maaa! Goats like to run and jump around.

Chickens

Farmers that keep chickens enjoy **fresh eggs** almost every day. Most chickens walk around outside during the day but **sleep** in a **hen house** at night to keep them safe.

A female chicken is called a hen. Her babies are chicks.

Chicks are so cute!

6

A male chicken is called a cockerel. He shouts "cock-a-doodle-doo"!

Hen egg

Duck egg

Goose egg

Other birds such as ducks and geese lay eggs as well, and so do some reptiles such as frogs and lizards.

Only female chickens lay eggs.

Hatching chick

Make your own picture collage of an egg becoming a chicken.

You will need:

Scissors
White, yellow, and red card
Cardboard tube
Acrylic paint
Paper
Glue
Feathers
Googly eyes

1

Ask an adult to cut two ovals from white card, one oval from yellow card, and a few thin strips from a cardboard tube.

2

Dip your hand in the paint and press it onto paper to create a chicken shape. Ask an adult to cut it out for you.

3

Ask an adult to cut out a jagged yellow rectangle, a red crown, two red triangles, and a red diamond from card.

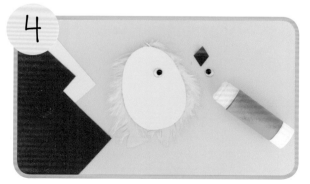

4

Fold the diamond in half. Glue the card, googly eyes, and the feathers in place. Use the page opposite as a guide.

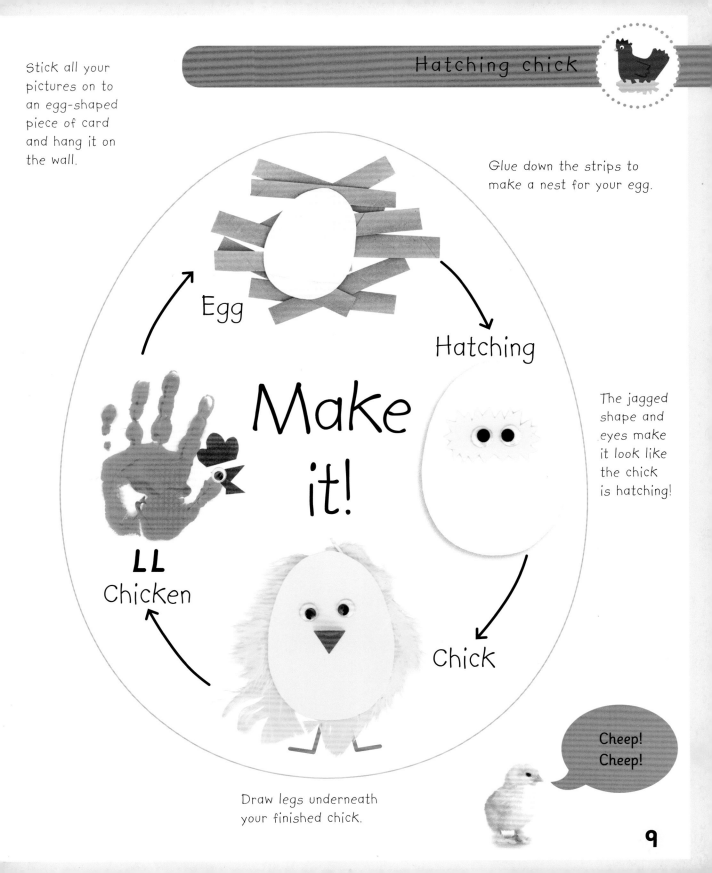

Stick all your pictures on to an egg-shaped piece of card and hang it on the wall.

Glue down the strips to make a nest for your egg.

Egg

Hatching

The jagged shape and eyes make it look like the chick is hatching!

Make it!

LL
Chicken

Chick

Draw legs underneath your finished chick.

Cheep! Cheep!

9

Counting sheep

Sheep are playful, social animals that are kept for both their **wool** and their **milk**. A group of sheep is called a **flock**.

A female sheep is called a ewe.

1

2

3

Flocks

Sheep don't like to be alone. They are much happier when they live as a group.

4

Baby sheep are called lambs.

Baaa

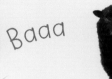

Did you know?

Some people say that counting sheep in your head can help you to fall asleep!

How many sheep can you count?

7

Baaa

6

5

Woolly coats

Every year or so, a sheep's fleece (their coat) is cut off and turned into wool. Not only is this useful, but doing it keeps the sheep from getting too hot.

9

Sheep come in lots of patterns and colours.

10

Baaa
Baaa

Sheepdogs

Lots of farms use a clever dog to gather up and move the flock of sheep around. This is known as "herding".

Fluffy sheep

It's really easy to create your very own **cute and fluffy** sheep. How many will there be in your **flock?**

You will need:
Cardboard
Scissors
Felt
Wool
Sticky tape

Don't forget to make a black sheep too!

1

Ask an adult to cut big and small rectangles out of cardboard. Wrap the rectangles with sticky tape.

2

Wrap a length of wool around the cardboard lots of times until it's thick and fluffy.

3

Bend the cardboard in the middle and carefully slide the cardboard out. You'll be left with the sheep's body.

4

Tie another piece of wool around the middle of the ball and pull it tight.

5

Ask an adult to do the cutting.

Cut around the edges of the ball, then fluff it out to finish the sheep's body.

6

Have an adult trim the wool to make it neat. Stick on felt and googly eyes for the face.

Baaa

Ducks

Farmers keep **ducks** for their **eggs**. Ducks love the **water**, and hang around in groups called **paddlings**.

Did you know?

Male ducks are called drakes. They are usually a lot more colourful than female ducks.

Eggs

Female ducks lay eggs and sit on them to keep them warm. Baby ducks are called ducklings.

Quack! Quack!

Flying south

Ducks are great fliers, and travel to warm places when it gets too cold. They fly together in a "V" shape, which makes it less windy for the ducks at the back.

Ducks have webbed feet so they can paddle and swim. This is why they waddle when they walk!

Cows

These big, useful animals can be found on **lots of farms**. **Cows** are sociable and usually quite friendly.

Mooo

Both male and female cows can have horns.

Grazing

Cows are very hungry animals! They spend most of their time in big green fields eating lots and lots of grass. This is known as "grazing".

Baby cows are called calves.

Milk

Many farms keep cows for their milk. We drink the milk and use it to make food such as cheese and ice-cream.

Cows raised for their milk are called "dairy cows".

Male cows are called bulls. They are big and strong.

Herds

Like sheep, cows are social animals that like to be with their friends and family in large groups called herds.

Mooo
Mooo

17

Milkshakes

Milk is a **tasty** treat on its own, but it's **even better** when it's made into a **shake.**

You will need:
Strawberries
Milk
Blender

Wash the strawberries and pull off the green stalks.

Pop the strawberries in a blender, then take the milk out of the fridge.

Sip and slurp your milkshake!

3

4

Pour the milk into a blender and ask an adult to blend the ingredients for 2–3 minutes until they have mixed together.

Pour the strawberry milkshakes into glasses. Grab a straw and enjoy!

What a pigsty

Some pigs live in orchards and forests.

Pigs are **clever** and **curious** animals. They live in **sties** with their friends and love to roll in mud.

Cooling off

Though they may look dirty, pigs are clean animals. They need to roll around in mud to keep cool and protect their skin from the sun. The mud stops them getting sunburned!

Did you know?

Some people keep mini pigs as pets!

Pigs are surprisingly good swimmers.

20

Pigs are as intelligent as some dogs.

Yum yum! Pigs love eating meat and plants.

A female pig is called a sow and a male pig is a boar. Their babies are called piglets.

Pigs are not just pink. They can be brown or black and white.

Snouts help them to smell and find food.

Who's my mum?

Do you know what these **baby farm animals** will grow up to be? Follow the footprints to match them to their **mums**.

Baby chickens are called **chicks**.

Baby pigs are called **piglets**.

Baby sheep are called **lambs**.

Baby ducks are called **ducklings**.

22

Help the babies find their parent.

Chicken
My babies like to say "Cheep! Cheep! Cheep!"

Sheep
My babies are covered in fluffy wool.

Pig
My babies love playing in the mud!

Duck
My babies love to go swimming.

Animal cookies

Looking for a **yummy treat?**
Try these delicious cookies shaped
like your **farmyard friends.**

You will need:
125 g (4½ oz) butter
125 g (4½ oz) caster sugar
1 egg yolk
1 tbsp honey
175 g (6 oz) plain flour
1 tsp cinnamon

1

Cream the butter and caster
sugar together in a bowl, then
mix in the egg yolk and honey.

2

Sift the flour and cinnamon on
top of the mixture to make
sure you don't get any lumps.

3

Mix the dough until it forms
a ball, then wrap in clingfilm
and chill for 30 minutes.

Cheep

Cheep

Decorate with writing icing

Baa

Moo

Oink

Neigh

4

Preheat the oven to 180°C (350°F/Gas 4). Roll out the dough so it's 5mm (¼ in) thick.

5

Cut out the cookies using the cookie cutters and place them on a non-stick baking sheet.

6

Ask an adult to bake the cookies for 12–15 minutes or until golden. Cool on a rack.

Horsing around

Humans have a special friendship with **horses**. They are **useful**, **strong** and **clever**.

Foals are often born at night.

Horseshoes

Metal shoes protect horses' hooves when they walk on hard roads.

Male horses are called stallions and females are called mares. Baby horses are called foals.

Working horses can do lots of jobs. They can carry heavy loads, pull carts, plough the land, and take people to and from places.

Ponies are a type of small horse.

Galloping

Horses walk, trot, canter and gallop. Galloping is when they run at full speed. People called jockeys race horses in competitions.

Horses can jump high!

Goats

Goats are **tough** but **playful** animals. Farmers use their **milk** and **hair**. They can live almost anywhere.

More people drink goats milk than cows milk. It is full of healthy vitamins.

A mummy goat recognizes her kid by its bleat!

Maaa!

Baby goats are called kids.

Horns

Some goats have horns. They like to butt horns to play, fight, or move someone out of the way!

28

Did you know?

Goats are fantastic climbers. They can easily climb trees and mountains.

Sticking together

Goats like living in big groups. Almost every group has a head female and a head male goat.

Keeping dry

Most goats don't like water, and run for shelter if it rains.

Goats will jump over puddles to avoid them!

29

Model farm

Making your own mini **farm** is so much **fun**. Where will all the **animals** go?

A little horse wants to enter the farm!

Neigh! Quack! Baa!

Cut a pond shape from blue paper.

Where's our mud?

30

1

Paint the *back* and *inside* of your box *blue*, then paint the *bottom green* and the *top* any colour you like. Leave to dry.

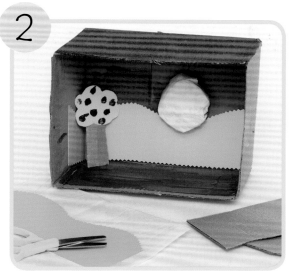

2

Ask an adult to cut shapes for your trees and hills. To make the Sun, scrunch yellow paper into a ball and glue it to the back.

3

Get an adult to cut fun flowers and shapes in lots of different colours. Stick them on as pretty decorations.

4

Arrange the toy animals to set the scene. Place the box on green paper so it looks like grass.

Index

Acknowledgements

The publisher would like to thank the following for their kind permission to reproduce their photographs:

(Key: a-above; b-below/bottom; c-centre; f-far; l-left; r -right; t-top)

4 Fotolia: Eric Isselee (br). 5 Fotolia: Mari art (bcr). 16 Fotolia: Eric Isselee (bcl). 21 Fotolia: Anatolii (cr); Fotolia: Anatolii (c); Peter Anderson (c) Dorling Kindersley, Courtesy of Odds Farm Park, High Wycombe, Bucks (bl); Geoff Brightling (c) Dorling Kindersley, Courtesy of the Norfolk Rural Life Museum and Union Farm (tr). 26 Getty: Photodisc / Thomas Northcut (bl). 29 Geoff Dann (c) Dorling Kindersley, Courtesy of Cotswold Farm Park, Gloucestershire (tl); Peter Anderson (c) Dorling Kindersley, Courtesy of Odds Farm Park, High Wycombe, Bucks (cr).

All other images © Dorling Kindersley
For further information see: www.dkimages.com

Thanks to Lucy Claxton for picture library assistance.